This book is dedicated to the salesperson inside of you that's dying to unleash itself on an unsuspecting world.

Introduction

I love selling.

I know that's a strange sentence to read for most of you, but it's the gospel truth. Nothing makes me happier than matching up a customer with a product or service that they will find useful, enjoyable and beneficial to their life/business.

My name is David Anderson. Most people simply call me Dave. No, I'm not the Dave Anderson who lends his name to a chain of "Famous" Barbecue Restaurants. I'm the Dave Anderson who sells.

Of course, I've sold under a lot of different titles: Radio Personality, YouTube Vlogger, Author, Motivational Speaker, Trainer, Consultant, Branding and Marketing Expert, Comedian, Minister, Husband, Son, Nephew, Cousin, Brother, Friend. No matter the title, or which hat I'm wearing, I'm always selling.

Having spoken to over one million people from the stage in my career, I understand that most people think they can't sell in order to make an impact. They are wrong! If a smart-ass jokester like me can sell, ANYONE can! They just need the right system in place and the willingness to adapt a different mindset.

Whether you choose to admit it or not, you are a

salesperson, and I can prove it:

Have you ever convinced someone to go on a date with you?

Have you ever gotten a loved one to get you something you REALLY wanted for your birthday, or just because?

Have you ever changed someone's mind about something they believed before you gave them your point of view?

Have you ever had consensual sex?

If you answered "yes" to at least one of those questions, congratulations…

You are a salesperson.

Now sit back, relax and let me show you how to sell without being like a "used-car salesman."

Let me show you how to Pitch, Close, Upsell and Repeat!

Chapter One:
The Art of the Pitch

As a product of divorced parents, I saw two different takes on entrepreneurship.

My father, Carl Anderson, a product of the military and law enforcement, believed in an action-oriented approach to business. He always seemed to weigh the probabilities of success over failure. To the outside world, my dad may have seemed like he painted outside the lines. The truth is that my father painted abstract works of art by the numbers.

When I was about seven years old, my father converted a building into a corner store with his brothers in the neighborhood where they grew up. For several years, they were a rarity in the Black community: A Black-owned corner store that charged reasonable prices and even gave credit to people who didn't have a lot of money for groceries.

There were things my father did that I didn't understand as a seven-year-old. One blistery summer day, a large truck pulled in front of my family's store. Soon, two men emerged from the truck and wheeled out an arcade game. I think it might have been Ms. Pac-Man. (Keep in mind that in this point in history, most kids, especially low- to middle-class kids, didn't have parents who could afford an Atari or Nintendo and Sega didn't have gaming systems yet, so arcade games were a big deal in the 1980s.) I was confused as to why one was being placed in a store, so I gathered my courage and tugged at my father's arm and asked, "Dad, why are you putting an arcade game in the store?"

My father, a six foot five, three hundred pound mountain of a man, smiled down at me and said, "That video game is going to bring in kids like you who want to play video games, my boy! There's no arcade around here, so this will bring kids from all around the neighborhood. They will ask their parents for money for the games and for snacks.

"Nine times out of ten," he continued, "their parents are going to also give them money for groceries to pick up little things for the house. Sometimes, my boy, you have to bait the trap if you want to eat."

To be honest, I didn't understand all of what that meant. As a man, I now see the brilliance in his thinking. My father wasn't what you would consider an "educated" man, but what he lacked in parchment and letters behind his name, he more than made up for in determination, common sense and vision. That business earned my family the seed money to expand to event catering. My uncle George was a five star chef, so it made use of his talents, and it made even more money. Although my father and uncles are no longer with me, their examples of entrepreneurship are alive in me today.

My mom, Edythe Anderson, on the other hand, is a very educated woman. As a model, teacher and cosmetologist, she's had varied experiences that have constantly challenged her and motivated her to go beyond her perceived capabilities. While she wasn't born with a silver spoon her mouth, my mother knew the importance of working for what you wanted and needed in this world.

My mother has done some amazing things that I've witnessed firsthand. From running the largest hair salon in Philadelphia at the time, to selling handmade jewelry at a 500% profit margin, my mother has a hustle and a fire inside of her that defies logic.

When I was fifteen, my mother bought a salon not too far from where she grew up. What I loved about my mother's salon, affectionately named "Girlfriends," was that it was cozy and warm. She named it Girlfriends because she wanted a place where friends could come and enjoy each other's company without the ears of meddling men or judgmental people with a different frame of reference.

Girlfriends was a full-service salon that not only

focused on quality hairstyling at an affordable price, but you could also get your nails done by a professional manicurist. Women of all ages had a place to come and feel relaxed and pampered while getting the full-service treatment. While that might not seem like an innovative concept today, in the early 1990s, it was unheard of, especially in the hood.

My mom was what I'd consider to be a calculated risk taker. She kept working as a teacher in the Philadelphia Public School District during the day and ran the salon in the evenings. When I asked her why she wouldn't give up teaching to pursue her passion full time, she said to me, with a small curl of a smile at the end of her lips, "David, you and your brother eat like runaway slaves! There's got to be a second income or otherwise we're going to be in trouble!"

My brother, Aaron, and I were two big guys and a huge burden for my mother growing up. Mom made sure we had exactly what we needed and didn't have the luxury of being frivolous. Although my mother let the salon go because of the enormous amount of wear and tear on her body, she never stopped having a second source of income. Even today, in the midst of her well-deserved retirement, my mother makes beautiful handmade greeting cards that are so nice, you'd never throw them away. They are small pieces of art that make for an excellent conversation starter. (Personally, I feel she doesn't charge nearly enough for them, but she's happy and that's all that matters.)

Though my parents had different philosophies, their intentions were to be successful and to serve the customer in a way that their services were top of mind. This is a key point that most people in business miss. It's the ability to make an offer to customers without the customer being consciously aware that they are being sold. This is the art of the Pitch.

What is a Pitch?

A pitch is a planned (well-thought-out) presentation of a product or service designed to initiate and close a sale of the same product or service. A sales pitch is essentially designed to introduce a product or service to an audience who knows nothing about it, or it is a descriptive expansion of a product or service that an audience has already expressed interest in.

A great pitch should be provocative, exciting, and appear to solve the problem (either perceived or real) that the potential customers seem to have. Your pitch is a big part of what could make or break your sale. Whether on the phone, in a commercial, or door-to-door, your pitch is a critical piece of your sales puzzle that you can't afford to miss.

No matter how persuasively you talk, how successfully you utilize visual aids or how influentially you utilize non-verbal communication, none of these abilities truly take care of business in a sales pitch unless you really close the deal. This section takes a gander at how you can convey a sales pitch that not just wows prospective customers with your awesome skills, but makes them fill out a PO (purchase order) before you leave the building or hang up the phone.

When designing your pitch, these are questions that you should be asking yourself in order to close more sales:

What is the pain? - The "pain" is the problem that your product or service can solve.

Why should they buy from you? - Are you invested in their well-being? Do you care about their pain? What makes them a perfect candidate for what you sell? Why will your product or service be the only thing they need to solve their problem?

What is the Cost vs. the Value? - Think someone won't pay $1 million for a glass of water? Leave them alone and thirsty in the desert for three days! If the situation is dire enough and what you have is valuable enough, people won't care about the cost. That's because it's up to you to make the value obvious!

Things you Must do to have an Effective Pitch

Boycott Canned Presentations

I know you've heard this before, but it's a fact—you truly can't recycle a stale sales presentation anytime you need to convey a compelling pitch. The issue with utilizing a canned presentation is that the center is on you—your organization, your item, your peculiarities and your profits. To truly interface with a prospect, you need to make it about **them**—**their** issues, **their** needs, **their** organization and **their** circumstance. Regardless of how earth-shatteringly awesome your product or service is, nobody's going to purchase it unless it's significant to their business.

Dig Deep and Keep Digging

Alright, we've made it clear that you have to tailor your pitch for the circumstances, now how would you go about it? Get on the telephone (or email) and begin asking your potential clients questions. What are their needs? What issues do they want to understand with your item? Is there any foundation data that you could utilize? What different arrangements would they say they are considering? Get some information about everything, without exception, that may be pertinent. Keep in mind, the vast majority will just provide for you a wide diagram of the circumstances. You need to truly burrow on because you want to reveal the motivation behind why your item/administration is the answer for their issue. This is what I refer to as "Discovery."

Tailor the Pitch for the Customer

When you have this data, now is the right time to make your presentation. Take their issue and transform it into a target that distinguishes a shared objective for you and your client. Accomplishing this goal ought to be the focal subject of your presentation. Case in point, if you're offering weight loss supplements, ask probing questions about the prospect's daily eating and exercise activities so you can address their shortcomings. In the event that their main issue is that they don't like cardio and salads, your pitch ought to concentrate on attempting to infuse subtle changes in their diet and level of exercise. When you find their main pain point and a secondary pain point, the end of your pitch should focus on how the supplements can help them achieve their goals along with decisive action on their part.

Be a Master Storyteller

A powerful approach to truly make your presentation resound with the people is to coordinate a story into your pitch. People adore genuine stories, so give them a story built around a customer who had a similar problem and the measures they took to conquer those hurdles (pointing out how your item saved the day).

Your story ought to be energizing, emotive (yes, it is possible and NECESSARY whether you're offering information-based products or selling bottled water on the side of the road on a hot summer day) and important to the current situation. For instance, if you're offering instructive programming, you could recount the story of an academically struggling school who introduced your product and in the very next year, 10% of the graduating class got full-ride scholarships to the school of their choice (you get the point). Conversely, in the case that you're offering tailored framework (fill in the blank, paint by number) segments, give an example of a similar firm who bought your framework, expanded productivity by 68%, and turned into the business-sector pioneer in their field.

Be sure your story is important to your target audience's interests—otherwise it could come off like you're boasting about past triumphs as opposed to convincing a future client that your product or service is something that their business can't thrive without. This is key to making your pitch effective.

Watch your "Pitch"!

One thing that people neglect in selling is their pitch. I'm not talking about their sales pitch, I'm talking about their *tone!*

Sometimes it's not *WHAT* you say, but *HOW* you say it. Moreover, I think that we miss out on the importance of non-verbal communication. Prospects pay attention to the way you look, the way you speak, your eye movements and more. I remember a colleague telling me that he lost a sale because the prospect didn't like his shoes. It is my strong belief that you have to be on point in every single aspect of your pitch.

Your pitch starts from the second your prospect answers the phone, or when you show up to meet them. I don't have a lot of time, and because every second is precious to me, I have no problem turning down a salesperson who is five minutes late. Time is money, and I feel as though my time should be respected. As you move forward in business, you will find that there are a lot of things that can turn someone off before you even open your mouth.

Speaking of mouths, please watch your hygiene! I'm not being funny when I say that. You can be the most talented salesperson in the world, but if I can't get past your funky breath or the glare from a mouth full of yellow teeth, you certainly won't be getting my business!

Mojo Up!

Have you ever heard that both dogs and bees can smell fear? The truth of the matter is that your prospects can smell your fear as well! Nerves can cost you the sale. Prospects will read nervousness as a sign of a shifty salesperson. The reason those of us who sell worry so much is that no matter how much we prepare, we are not in control of the reaction of the prospect to our offer. Every pitch is a potential payday, so you have got to make sure you go into every pitch with the right mindset. In other words, you need to Mojo UP!

To Mojo UP is to find that space in your mind where your skills, knowledge, talent and charm come together in order to put you in the best position to close the sale from the moment you begin. My best way to Mojo UP is to listen to a song that puts me in the mood to conquer the world and DOMINATE my prospect! You need an anthem! My anthem is "Cult of Personality" by Living Colour. It gets me amped and makes me feel like I can do anything that I set my mind to!

Another way to Mojo UP is to know your product or service backwards and forward. If you think that it's not that important and that all you should do is just sell the way that "everyone else" sells, watch an episode of ABC's *Shark Tank*.

If you've never seen it, *Shark Tank* is a show that is all about Pitching. Hopeful entrepreneurs offer millionaire and billionaire investors an equity stake in their company in exchange for a certain amount of cash to help expand or grow their businesses. If the investors don't agree to the proposed pitch, the entrepreneurs walk away with nothing.

They don't call these folks sharks for nothing. When someone starts to pitch, you can see the interest or disgust on the faces of the sharks based on the information presented to them. When the sharks begin to ask for facts and figures, or go into a line of questioning that the entrepreneur isn't prepared to answer, the sweat forms, which at this point, might as well be blood in the water. Many a business owner has felt the bite of a money hungry shark who hates having their time wasted by an unprepared poser.

This is the sentiment of your prospect when you don't know everything there is to know about your product or service. You look like a fraud, a phony, a fake, a liar and a clueless poser. Simply put, your presentation is over before you start unless you know EVERYTHING there is to know about your offer. At bare minimum, you had better know much more than your prospect.

When you have this information etched into your brain, then you can focus on more important things, like the body language of your prospect and the things that interest/concern your prospect.

Pitching ain't Easy

Keep in mind that pitching, like any specialized skill, is an art form. Everyone will use whatever unique style works for them. Even if you aren't the best salesperson, you must put in the time to perfect your craft. You can be a lot of things in sales. However, if you're not a great pitcher, all hope of you having a great career in sales is lost.

A great pitcher knows what the customer is looking for

and how they need to be sold. A great pitcher is part P.T. Barnum, part Mister Rogers and a lot of Steve Jobs. You have to be bigger than life, extremely loving, patient and understanding. Above all else, you must be able to excite people about the possibility of a better life experience because of what you're offering them.

Steve Jobs, the revolutionary leader behind Apple's dominance of the tech industry, understood this from every imaginable angle. Whenever there was a product to be announced, Jobs held a very unique press conference. While other CEOs would dress up, Jobs wore the same outfit every time: a black shirt, a pair of blue jeans and sneakers or a very sensible pair of shoes. This made you feel like he was a normal guy that was just there to show you something cool.

Steve Jobs was one of the greatest salesmen in the history of the world. He understood that while modern technology makes life more convenient, it can be challenging to get people to embrace it. Jobs made people feel like they needed to have whatever iGadget he was pushing. This first real perfect pitch came when Apple was to introduce the iPod for the first time.

The world was a very different place in 2001. Five weeks before, the United States experienced the worst terrorist attack in its history. People were scared to shop because they didn't know if 9/11 was an isolated incident or just the precursor of darker things to come. Many people began to stop buying CDs in favor of file sharing services like Napster. The talent it takes to get people to buy songs during a time when illegal music downloads and fear were at an all-time high is incredible, but Jobs did just that.

First, Jobs stated the problem, that current mp3 players were flimsy, portable CD players were bulky and that almost no one listened to a full album anymore. That's when he gave them a solution in a language that everyone from ages eight to eighty could understand. He told the audience that the iPod would put "One thousand songs in your pocket." At that point the entire world began buzzing and Jobs had effectively made everything that came before the iPod obsolete. He repeated this simple but massively effective pitch with several Apple products and irreversibly changed the world and how tech companies approach consumers.

What does your pitch look like? Do you understand how to convey a message simply and directly, while providing enough information to educate your prospects? Can you give people a show and entertain them? Do you know how to warm up your prospects? Do you have a pitching style, or can you adapt on a dime to match the temperament of your prospects?

Before I get into the best pitch I feel you can give, I want to show you several pitches that people tend to use in sales these days.

5 Types of Pitches

1. *The Curiosity Pitch*

The curiosity pitch is all about giving the prospect a point of intrigue. You want them to ask you for more by putting them in the position to care about what you *might* have to offer.

Example: (Private car service salesperson)

Salesperson: *"Hey! Wouldn't it be nice if you never had to drive to work again?"*

Prospect: *"Yeah, that would be nice. But then how would I get to work?"*

This is when you move into your presentation.

2. *The 10:00 News Pitch*

If you've ever watched the news, you know that in most cases the news is more of a show than actually a source of relevant topics that are important to you. So this pitch is used to scare people.

Example: (Door-to-door cleaning product salesperson)

Salesperson: *"Did you know that over one thousand different infection-causing microorganisms are lurking in your home? What are you doing about that?"*

Prospect: *"No. Where would they be?"*

Salesperson: *"Everywhere! Let me show you."*

3. **The Strangé Pitch**

Strangé is a character played by Grace Jones in the 1992 Eddie Murphy movie *Boomerang*. She was bold and didn't believe in taking no for an answer. She was almost a bully, preying upon people and their weaknesses and insecurities. I could have called this "The Suge Knight Pitch" but I thought this was more creative (and a lot less violent).

Salesperson: YOU NEED THIS *(PRODUCT/SERVICE)*! WHAT ARE YOU WAITING FOR? YOU SAID YOU HAVE *(A PROBLEM THAT YOUR PRODUCT/SERVICE WILL SOLVE)*, SO YOU NEED TO GET THIS NOW!!!"

Customer: **Speechless** Usually the customer runs for the hills and will never buy from you if you use this approach. No one wants to be bullied into giving you their hard-earned money. I totally believe in being direct, persistent and consistent, but being intimidatingly aggressive is not something I will ever endorse.

You may think it's ridiculous that anyone would ever

act that way during the course of a pitch, but you would be surprised. Imagine if you hadn't sold anything, or if you missed your quota. If you didn't have an actionable and repeatable procedure to get sales, you'd be desperate. Unfortunately, desperate times call for desperate measures. Desperate measures lead to failure. (Note, The only time this works is when you know that the prospect is really going to buy but wants you to work for the business.)

4. **The Twitter Pitch**

This is pretty much exactly what it sounds like: A pitch that gets whittled down to 140 characters or fewer. I wouldn't recommend this unless you can do it in a way that shows your knowledge of the product or service and also your self-confidence.

This pitch is more of an exercise that I find is useful for trimming the fat (excess and unnecessary words) from your sales presentation. If you have a lot to say on twitter, you usually have to chop it down in order for it to fit within 140 characters. You should definitely find a way to be impactful with fewer words as opposed to being unconvincing with more words.

5. **Email Subject Line Pitch**

Some of the best pitches in the world happen in the inbox. The same way that a pitch gets you in the door when you're in person or a good pitch will set an appointment on the phone, that's what an email subject line should do. Here are a couple of examples:

If you're not using (name of product/service), you're missing out on (solution your product/service provides)!

Hey (Customer Name)! Here's how I (Achieved success your product/service provides) in (short amount of time).

Tired of NOT (insert customer's major problem)?

99% Of People Fail Because (Insert reason for industry failure). Here's How
You Can Join The Elite 1% :

Get Real Results With (product name)

STOP! This Is The Most Important Letter You've Read All Day…Read On To Discover How You Can Achieve (Insert customer's biggest dream).

The object of the game is to entice your prospect and get them curious enough to open your email and then take action on your offer.

The Way That I Pitch

I believe that the pitch is truly an art form that needs to be as fluid as possible. While it's hard to write, it's basically a matter of preparation.

I look at every possible factor that could hinder me connecting with the prospect. Then I come up with every possible way to remove any point of inconvenience. For example, if a prospect says they are in a meeting and they are running over into our meeting time, I will wait for them. I don't believe in rescheduling. Rescheduling is a sales killer. It gives the prospect too much time to "think."

If the prospect says that they can't make it or their car has broken down, I will meet them where they are and call my AAA Roadside service to handle their vehicle while we discuss business. This shows the prospect that you care about more than just getting their hard-earned money. It also shows the prospect that you are passionate about your product or service and that you will go beyond the call of duty.

In my less than humble opinion, your introduction will make or break you. With most prospects, you have at most two sentences to establish enough trust to get them to listen to whatever it is you have to offer.

I believe the best pitches are done face-to-face because you leave very little room for misinterpretation. You also get to read the prospect's body language and see firsthand what makes them tick.

When pitching in person, I always smile. I smile to the point where it becomes infectious. Recently, I went into a company that was interested in having me represent their digital sales products. When they grilled me, I sat there, answering each and every one of their questions with a smile and a positive attitude. Twenty minutes later, I walked out of that meeting with the contract.

Making sure that you keep your demeanor confident, warm and trustworthy will instantly allow you to establish authority with your prospect. With that, I always make sure that if I happen to pause, it's for effect and not because I am reaching for what to say next.

One thing that I need to stress to you is the importance of **shutting the hell up!** I see so many salespeople of all ages talk themselves out of a deal that should have been a slam dunk, because they talked the customer out of a deal. My father would call this "snatching defeat from the jaws of victory."

People tend to talk too much when they are desperate to close a sale and inadvertently wind up giving the prospect a reason to doubt and or hesitate on making a purchase. It's totally okay to use a selling point in order to accent your pitch, but if your pitch is full of selling points (*e.g., This flux capacitor will get you to the past and back to the future. You'll also have access to the 1.21 jiggawatts and this will fit perfectly in the Delorean*) you will talk your way out of a sale. A good product or service doesn't require a lot of hyping up because its value should be evident.

The more naturally you carry yourself, the more luck you'll have when it comes to pitching. I don't care where I am, I automatically put myself in the mindset of being at home. This automatically calms my mind and diminishes my nervousness, allowing me to focus on giving the prospects a quality product or service that is going to drastically improve their lives. This should be your goal beyond anything else, including money. Money is a byproduct of you delivering your quality product or service. Your pitch should always be positioned to help the customer first, beyond any personal financial gain. This should be evident whether you're in front of the customer or on the phone.

The Art of the Cold Call

As an effective salesperson entrepreneur, you have to understand that the cold call is fundamental and unavoidable if your goal is success. No matter what your needs are in business—more customers, an investor, an advance or advice, you will need to get to the correct individual, stand out just enough to be noticed and persuade them to make a move in your direction.

When I first started in business, nobody knew me. Those who did only knew me as a radio personality and entertainer. I basically had no cold calling experience, however I did (and still do) have a considerable measure of guts and I knew I didn't want to be poor. I made over one thousand cold calls a week and caught up with key individuals who had hung up on me days prior. Although I got my ass handed to me more than I thought I would between making sales—if I can cold call, be cursed out and not be adversely affected, I could conquer anything!

In order to do anything on an expert level, I believe that you should turn yourself into a student of what it is you're trying to master. The only way for me to become the best at selling was to learn how to sell anything and everything. What I did over the course of six years isn't for the faint of heart, but it made me the salesman I am today. So what did I do? I took sales jobs in industries I knew nothing about.

When I say that I sold everything, I mean I. Sold. EVERYTHING. It was not easy at all, but it allowed me some amazing experiences that I still carry with me to this day.

One of the first industries where I tried my luck was in home security sales. In this industry, I worked at two companies: Honeywell and ADT.

My Honeywell experience was very enlightening to say the least. First, the owner of the branch was a very quirky character who only went by "Z." At first glance, you'd think that Z was just some country bumpkin, with huge cowboy boots and a bigger belt buckle to match, who couldn't possibly have a handle on or mastery of business. You'd be wrong. Z not only understood sales, he understood people. Although it was Honeywell Home Security I was working for, Z was a self-made man. (FYI, home security companies sell equipment and branded materials to dealers who go out and sell and install the equipment on the company's behalf. It's almost like owning a restaurant franchise).

Z's model for running his business was something I'd never seen. First, he didn't believe in uniforms for his sales staff. He required shirts and ties at all times from the men and conservative dress from the women.

Every single day (minus the weekends) at 12:45 pm, there was a sales meeting. Z's idea of a sales meeting was very layered and served many purposes:

1.   To find out what appointments the staff had scheduled that day and what difficulties we were having
2.   To go over each staff member's sales pitch and critique it
3.   To talk strategy
4.   To motivate and inspire

Keep in mind, I've worked for Les Brown, so I consider myself an excellent judge of motivational speakers. Z was brilliant! He understood how to encourage those who were struggling and keep those of us who were excelling excited and challenged.

Here's the thing that was unheard of for me: Z never

provided anyone with leads. Not. One. Lead. EVER! Instead of giving us leads which may or may not be good or qualified, he had a system that would secure a 60% closing rate! In the Home Security industry (or almost any industry for that matter), that is an amazing success rate.

Here's the strategy:

First you have to go through all of your contacts and call them, explaining that you're working on getting your own branch once you hit a certain goal. All you need to do is to practice to perfect your pitch. This starts the cycle.

When you go to visit your friends and family, you go through your pitch (Z's pitch involved a picture book that did almost all of the selling for you) and ask them how they felt about the job you did. You take their feedback and then ask them their opinion on the product. If they like it and you're able to close them then that's great. More importantly is what comes next. This is where you start fishing for referrals.

As long as your friend likes the product, then you ask them the "winning question":

Who do you know in your circle who could benefit from having this level of service in their lives?

Normally, a person's first reaction is to say that they "can't think of anyone" they know, but they'll "get back to you" if they think of someone. The easiest way of combatting that is by what I call The Godfather Scenario.

The Godfather Scenario is exactly what you think it is… and then some! You give the customer an offer that they can't refuse, and then you up the stakes. This was the brilliant part of Z's plan. It sets you up to win. If you're a horrible salesperson, you can still get quality referrals while working on your pitch. If you are a good salesperson, this method is like a rocket booster.

For 3 referrals, the referrer would receive a gift certificate for $1,000 in groceries. (Yes, you read that right. One. Thousand. Dollars.)

When they provided 6 referrals, the referrer would receive a three night cruise for two that was redeemable for up to a year. (Airfare not included.)

At ten referrals, the referrer would receive a seven night cruise for two that was redeemable for up to a year. (Airfare not included.)

Somehow, Z found a company that would provide these certificates and they were completely legitimate!

Whenever you pitch anyone, you have to keep in mind that we live in a cynical world full of shitty salespeople who lie, cheat and steal in order to get the sale. I refer to those salespeople as pond scum.

Pond scum create cynicism, so that means you have to be willing to give up a piece of the pie in order to get potential referrers to move for you. Simply put, just give them some cash instead of gift certificates or knickknacks! What I would tend to do is give people enough money per referral who signed up that it would entice them to bring me multiple referrals. If you give them too little, most referrers won't waste their time working on your behalf. Conversely, if you give them too much, they will only work for that one payday and won't be a consistent source of quality referrals.

I have to admit, barring any complications (credit rating, lack of cash), when I used Z's system, I was closing everything in sight.

Another thing about working for Z was that he didn't allow you to be idle. "One A Day is a VITAMIN, not a goal," he'd say. This meant that without exception, you'd have to have at least three appointments on the books every single day. The reason that three appointments was mandatory is that most people will close at least one out of three appointments. What if you only had one appointment and you didn't close it? You would starve. Unfortunately, this meant having to cold call.

Cold calling is especially nerve-racking for most salespeople, especially door-to-door cold calling. I personally hated doing it because I don't like having doors slammed in my face or being cursed out, but I had to keep appointments on the books, so I had to get creative.

For me, creativity began with a visit to Ms. Bullock's daycare. The one thing I learned about daycare center owners is that they are the best kind of capitalist: the greedy kind. Owning a daycare business is great because you work limited hours and the daily operating costs are relatively low. Moreover, you are able to charge parents through the nose for taking care of their children. Simply put, daycare owners are about making money.

All I did was promise Ms. Bullock $50 for every person who got a system installed. After a few months, I never had to knock on a single door or ring anyone's bell to generate a lead. My commissions went through the roof and my referrals were insane.

Let's say that I ran into a day where I struck out (that was a rare occasion but it did happen from time to time). That wasn't a problem. I'd just go home and watch the news.

The news is a great source for finding prospects for whatever it is you sell. Since I was selling home security at the time, I would pay close attention to stories that focused on home invasions, burglaries, fires and kidnappings. I'd canvass the entire block and three or four blocks in either direction. Even if I was met with resistance, I'd say, "The only reason I'm here is because a guy got murdered (burglarized, injured in a fire, etc.) and he lives about six doors down from you. So if something like that ever happens again, you KNOW how slow the cops and the fire department can be." This usually got me the sale or a ton of referrals.

There are people who say they can't overcome objections. I say those people aren't creative enough. Here's what I mean:

There were times when I ran into people who already had a home security system. More often than not, they'd say they had an ADT system. At that time, many people couldn't afford to upgrade to their wireless system, and that's when my creativity kicked in.

I went to Home Depot and got myself a pair of $3 bolt cutters in anticipation of this very moment. Here's how my interaction with those customers went:

Me: *"I'm so glad you have at least some kind of protection in your home, but don't you know that ADT can't keep you safe?"*

Them: *"What do you mean? They're the biggest name in home security."*

Me: *"Bigger isn't always better. Your ADT system runs through a phone line, right?"*

Them: *"Yeah, so?"*

Me: *"So what happens if I'm a burglar/killer/bad guy and I have a pair of these? Haven't you seen the movies where someone is getting captured? The first thing the bad guy does is cut the phone wire!"*

Them: *"Oh..."*

Me: *"My system is wireless, so cutting the phone line means nothing. It also has a two-way system in it so our monitoring center can hear everything that happens in real time. And it's cheaper than that DEATH TRAP you've got hanging on your wall."*

Them: *"Really? How much?"*

Me: *"Just forty-nine dollars a month including installation and removal of that Automatic Death Trap or ADT for short!"*

While you might be shaking your head in disbelief, it was that pitch and that determination that got me a lucrative sales contract with ADT to sell their brand-new wireless system. I used these tactics at ADT, which also had much better marketing and resources, and made a killing. My job became a dream! But with every dream comes a wake-up call! Although I was selling a similar product, my time at ADT was a different experience with a different set of circumstances.

I had a manager named Jacob who quite frankly was the biggest jerk I'd ever worked for in my entire career. He wanted me to sell in a way that was foreign to me and hindered my creativity. Sometimes you have to be so results driven that your supervisor's rules don't matter.

With ADT you get a certain number of leads/appointments that come from the company's marketing efforts, but the rest need to come from SGLs—Self Generated Leads. If you didn't get at least five or more SGLs per month, Jacob would pull those leads away from you.

At Honeywell, I had flexibility and gift certificates to bargain with. At ADT I only had cash, which could take up to four weeks to get to a referrer. The system was problematic for me, and I was looking like a superstar ball player from the minor leagues who couldn't hack it in the majors.

I had to find a way to get my mojo back. I had about four days before I would be at Jacob's mercy and he'd pull away my leads. I found myself in North Philadelphia one day, just a stone's throw away from my old alma mater, Temple University.

I was amazed at how the area had changed in such a few short years. Where so much blight and danger once stood, new glowing structures were popping up like daisies in springtime. Some things in an old neighborhood never change. One of them is the block mother.

The block mother is usually a term reserved for the oldest woman on the block in the hood. She lives either in her window or on her porch, observing the goings-on in the world around her. If you're having a hard time picturing this in your mind's eye, google "Pearl from 227."

While I walked around the neighborhood, I spotted a bunch of old homes that had recently started renovations. I realized that only a developer could be flipping so many properties in order to profit off of a mass influx of Temple students who don't want to live in the dorms. (As a person who lived in those dorms, I can't say that I blame them! The bathrooms can be disgusting! LOL).

I knew at this point I had a problem that I needed to solve and the developer(s) would be an instant solution. If anybody would know how to track down the developer, the block mother would. It was time for me to "cold call."

I saw the block mother sitting on her perch on her porch. I simply introduced myself.

Me: *"Good morning, Ma'am! How are you?"*

Block Mother: *"Blessed and highly favored, baby! What you doing?"*

Me: *"I grew up not too far from here. My mom taught school down the street and I graduated from Temple. I* saw that there's a lot of renovation going on and I was wondering if you ever saw the developer who bought all of these old houses."

Block Mother: *"Sure have! He's right around the corner. What are you selling?"*

Me: *"I work for ADT so I do home security. Do you have a system in your home?"*

Block Mother: *"Yes indeed. The boy you're looking for is around the corner. You can't miss him."*

Me: *"Thanks so very much. I will see you when I come back."*

Block Mother: *"Alright, baby."*

When I got around the corner, I realized what the Block Mother meant by "you can't miss him." It's rare that you see a short Ukrainian man named German in a predominantly Black neighborhood, especially one that's known for violence and robbery. I walked up to him, introduced myself, and told him where I was from, and what happened next was nothing short of awesomeness.

German: *"So I have about thirty units. Can you cut me a volume deal? If you can, I've got 10 other properties that could use a wireless system."*

Me: *"Of course I can cut you a volume deal (meaning*

I could give him a discount because he was getting so many units installed). I just need to run back to my car and get more paperwork."

On my way back to the car, I stopped to thank Mrs. Jenkins, the Block Mother. I stepped right on her porch, hugged her and thanked her profusely. I also reached into my pocket and gave her $50. Her help wound up putting another $100,000 in business in my pocket, so she deserved that $50.

The funny thing about my coworkers at ADT was that they always did exactly what they were told. They would go to see realtors and try to see if they could get listings on new home buyers, or spend six hours a day canvassing neighborhoods, hoping to sell one alarm system. That's not for me. If I'm going to cold call— whether on the phone or in person—I'm going to approach it strategically.

Even today, I still need to cold call in my business! Here are the six key approaches to go about it effectively:

1. ***Certainty is key***. Be sold on what you bring to the table so much that it would be dishonest not to enlighten the prospect regarding it. I'm not kidding. Think about your service or product as an answer for their problem/need. "I trust I'm not annoying you" ought to be changed to "I have something that will help you make (or spare) more cash and rapidly affect your business."

2. ***Open with your purpose behind cold calling the prospect.*** It's about the client. "Michelle, this is Dave Anderson, and I'm calling/here today because…" Open with eagerness, excited about why you're cold calling. This helps to get you noticed without wasting time. Be clear and direct.

3. ***Make a Jurassic-sized claim at the beginning of the call/interaction.*** "The reason I am calling is to help you manage your money, bring down your debt and reveal to you an exclusive approach to build deals." If you aren't ready to make that enormous case with conviction, go home and reconvince yourself of your product or service.

4. ***Foresee questions, objections and complaints.*** You must have the capacity to anticipate each conceivable reaction from the individual you are calling. Make a rundown of conceivable reactions, inquiries, objections and protests with answers and rebuttals that you can offer instantaneously. You need to act as if you're some kind of sales psychic so that the potential customer knows that you're not in the business of playing around.

5. ***Keep up an incredible demeanor.*** On the off chance that your lead is impolite or cavalier, stay positive regardless. I get cold calls constantly at my office. My secretary accumulates data about clients to decide how best to help them. She's respectful and expert. I wasn't

accessible and one client got disappointed in light of the fact that they needed to talk with me specifically. He didn't get what he wanted, so he threw a tantrum and suddenly hung up. If that client kept up an incredible demeanor, he'd presumably have a greater chance winning over the staff and getting his objective fulfilled. Rather, he got nasty with my assistant and never got his goal accomplished.

6. *Be Artful, Articulate, Aggressive and Awesome*. I once had a kid cold call me daily when I worked as a Program Director at CBS Radio to land a part-time position. Each time he called, he was respectful and charming *(Artful)* to my receptionist and assistant. He was direct (not pushy) and made it clear *(Articulate)* that he wouldn't quit calling until he got to meet with me. By the third week *(Aggressive)*, anybody at my office who took his call knew who he was. He was so impressive *(Awesome)* that my own team was beginning to vouch for him. He won me over and is still working as a successful personality today. Utilization of the four A's has been instrumental in my success in business.

Cold calling is a skill that a successful entrepreneur must figure out how to ace. The sooner you begin to cold call as an approach to advance your business, the better off you will be. Set your targets ridiculously high, ten times higher than you would typically, and then get busy smiling and dialing. The more calls you need to make, the speedier you'll manage the rejection. Also, with each one of those calls you make, you have no time to get complacent.

Make Objections Your Bitch!

One thing that I have learned after spending over two-thirds of my life in sales is that people love to object. Most of the time, the objections are just an imaginary roadblock that prospects put up in order to justify buying a product or service from you.

Objections come up for three main reasons:

Smokescreens - These are basic responses that people use almost out of instinct. For example, if someone tells you at the start of your pitch that they aren't interested in your leaf removal service, but their front porch and their yard are covered in massive piles of freshly fallen leaves, you know that they are objecting for objection's sake.

Practicality - They can't see how using your product or service can serve them in their daily lives. If this objection comes up, what the prospect is asking you for is more information. It's up to you to show them how they can regularly benefit from what you have to offer.

Fear of Change - This kind of objection is usually from someone who enjoys the status quo. It's not that these prospects don't see the benefit, but there is a small section of the planet that lives to avoid change at all costs.

At this point, you may be asking, "Dave, what's the best thing to do when faced with any type of objection? Agree with the prospect. Lots of lackluster salespeople want to argue back and forth, and this is a bad move. Not only will you be wasting valuable selling time, but you'll most likely piss off the prospect.

Chapter Two:
The Art of the Close

Closing seems to be the one thing that most entrepreneurs struggle with the most. I've worked one-on-one with countless entrepreneurs on their sales process. Whether they are multimillionaires or in the startup phase of their business, most people seem to "clam up" when it comes to closing.

While we spend untold amounts of time trying to build our brands, products and services, we neglect the importance of complementing our pitches with effective closes. Without that one-two punch, you are most assuredly going to miss out on clients, profits and opportunities to grow your business.

So what does it mean to "close" a sale?

Closing a sale is literally the do-or-die moment in any sales presentation. It comes at the end of your pitch. As any top salesperson will tell you, a good close can snatch victory from the jaws of defeat. Unfortunately, a weak close can just as easily snatch defeat from the jaws of victory.

In this section, we'll go over the different types of closes and how these closes usually affect potential customers.

The Morpheus Close – This is a close where you give people two choices, like a red or blue pill. In this case, instead of one choice being an option to walk away, BOTH choices lead to a sale of some sort. Unfortunately, this isn't the Matrix and people may take offense to being forced to make a snap decision. The key to making this close work is to make both choices so compelling that the potential customer doesn't miss the option to say "no."

The Have a Baby Close – This close is inspired by the phrase "There's never a good time to have a baby." Primarily used by people who sell big ticket items, this close is totally about putting the potential purchase in perspective for the potential customer who may be on the fence. Its effectiveness depends on how solid a job you do in your pitch. If the potential customer has the money but may be fishing for a deal, sell the VALUE. If the customer is broke, this may be a difficult sale. Even still, sell the VALUE.

The Mulberry Bush close – I also call this one "The Punk Ass close." This is the one where the salesperson moves to the close with an indirect or soft (punk ass) question. "How do you feel about getting started?" or "How does this contract look to you?" The reason that this close is problematic is that it leaves way to many variables. Worse yet, it gives your prospect a reason (if not several reasons) to object and back out of the sale. When you beat around the bush with this type of close, you are putting yourself in a position of weakness and have given up all control of your interaction with the prospect. Always be direct, sure of yourself and in control at all times.

The "Spouse Consult Close" - When you've given a killer presentation and answered every question, sometimes the prospect will say something to the effect of *"I need to consult with my spouse before I make a decision."*

When someone says that to me, I usually respond with an agreement and then I deliberately hit them in the gut with their own logic. I'll say *"I always go over everything with my wife, so that makes a lot of sense. Normally before I head out to make a purchase, my spouse and I have already spoken about it. So would your spouse be surprised that you're here?"*

About 99% of the time, the prospect will say *"No. My spouse knows I'm here and we've talked about it."*

I will reply by saying *"Awesome! Let's get this off of your to-do list. Will you be paying with VISA, MasterCard, AMEX or Discover?"*

It's bold, but it lets them know that you aren't going to waste a lot of time getting caught up in their excuses. As a salesperson, you're there to get the job done and allow the prospect to get over their apprehension about improving their life with your product/service.

The Double Back Close - This is used only when you have a significant amount of hemming and hawing from the prospect. Instead of arguing, or getting stuck on closing, what you want to do is stress the benefits of your product or service and how they are perfectly matched to the needs or the pain of the prospect.

Say that your prospect is stuck on the price. This usually happens because they are either cheap or they can never say yes without haggling a salesperson.

Another sales coach would tell you to simply list the benefits of your product or service. I'm saying that you need to use everything you've learned in the discovery part of your pitch to close them. For example:

Me: *"Sir, I know you said that right now you are sick*

and tired of the dropped calls that are taking place with that phone you have. You said that it's a pain in the ass when you're trying to talk business. Did I understand that correctly?"

Prospect: *"Yeah... That's what I said."*

Me: *"Okay, so imagine how much money you've missed out in the last year by having that mediocre phone that you don't even like! I'm sure it would more than take care of the cost of the phone. You also have a thirty day money back guarantee. Before I give you your new phone (always attach ownership of the product or service to the prospect), I'm going to program my cell phone number in here. I want you to call me at any time, day or night, if you have the slightest problem with your phone."*

Prospect: *"Thanks so much!"*

Me: *"No problem. Now you said you wanted this in blue, so I've got the blue model all packed up for you. I just need your credit card and your old phone so I can do you the favor of tossing that piece of crap in the garbage for you."*

As long as you keep it conversational and use the information the prospect gives you, you're almost guaranteed to close that sale.

The I Feel Horrible Close - This close is so unfair to the prospect, but it gets them off of their nonsense and back onto the sale. I use this close to snatch victory from the jaws of defeat.

Me: *"Look. I feel horrible that I wasn't able to come to terms with you on this. I know that I tried my hardest and I thought I explained everything to you. Can you just let me know how I failed you? Was it something I did? Something I didn't do? Did I say something wrong? Was there something that I didn't say?"*

Prospect: *"No, Dave, you were great! You didn't do or say anything wrong."*

Me: *"Thanks so much! That sets my mind at ease. So since nothing's wrong, let's go ahead and get this done now. I know you don't have time to waste going through all of this again with someone else when it's obvious you need the product/service now. Let's get this done today and you can move on to more important matters."*

The I Can't Think Straight Close – This close is used

primarily to make the prospect believe that all you want to do is get them the best deal possible.

"You know, I will not be able to think straight until I get you exactly what you want. Until you feel like what we have to offer is worth the time, energy, and effort it requires to make this deal happen. Let me talk to my manager about giving you a better deal than what I initially presented."

Honestly, you won't be talking to your manager. The object of the game is to make the prospect feel as if you are going to be their advocate and giving them an even better deal than what they initially thought possible. This automatically shifts their mind from thinking of you as some kind of sleazy salesperson. With this close you automatically become a friend as well as an ally. You become what everyone needs: you become that person on the inside, fighting for their business.

The Referral Close - A rookie salesperson will tell you to ask for referrals at the end of the sale. The best time to ask for referrals is right after you've set up the value of the product or service you're selling. If you ask for referrals right before you close, the prospect will believe that you will owe them something. Simply put, it's a way to get them to believe that if you get referrals from them, they will get some kind of bonus or incentive in order to give you quality referrals that you could close.

"Now before we go any further I was just wondering, who do you know who could use or benefit from having this great quality product or service that I'm giving you today?"

More importantly, the best part about doing the referral close is that it assumes the sale for you. Most people are going to get referrals to something that they would use themselves, so this helps you assume the close for your product or service for this prospect.

The Drake Close - In the case that you are not familiar, Drake is a rap artist who coined the phrase Y.O.L.O., which stands for You Only Live Once.

The one thing that always, always frustrated me as a salesperson is that some prospects have the ridiculous belief that somehow you have to hoard money like you're Scrooge McDuck. Money comes in, money goes. There's a reason that it's referred to as *"Cash flow"* or *"Currency."*

If we're being honest with ourselves, we know for a fact that many people make ridiculous purchases all of the time. We also know that they have even more ridiculous reasons to justify those purchases. Millions of people stand in line just to get a new pair of Michael Jordan sneakers on the day that they come out. Middle-aged men go out and buy motorcycles because they are having a "midlife crisis." Never allow anyone to tell you that they can't justify the purchase because of cost. If they try, here's what you say to them:

"Now I know that this is not exactly a cheap purchase, but you know as well as I do that something cheap is never good and something good is never cheap. What I want you to understand is one simple fact about life: You will not get out of it alive, let alone with your money! Why not pay for the things that you really want that would give you the quality of life that you deserve? After all, you only live once."

Once the prospect realizes that they are definitely going to benefit from having your product or service, all you have to do is finish closing the deal by writing up the paperwork and/or taking their credit card information.

The Be a Leader Close - I only use this close when a prospect tries to tell me they can find a "comparable" product or service that can get the job done.

In order to be an effective salesperson, you have to be willing to put up a mirror to your prospects' faces and let them see the ugliness of their hesitation.

Me: *"So what I'm hearing you say is that you think that you can find a comparable product that will suit your needs. Is that correct?"*

Prospect: *"Yes. There's always a bargain out there."*

Me: *"You're absolutely right! So let me ask you something. If you know there are bargains, then why are you here?"*

Prospect: *"(silence, or) I just wanted to weigh my options."*

Me: *"Great, since you know that this is a more expensive option, you must obviously see the value in it. Otherwise you wouldn't be here in the first place. Let's go ahead and make this happen. You're a leader, and a leader places value over cost. Followers concern themselves with cost first, without thinking about the value. Be a leader, and let's make this happen."*

Nine times out of ten, if you hear this type of language come from a prospect, they're hoping that it'll send you into a panic and force you to do some kind of bargain type of deal for them. Do not fall for this. The problem is that savvy prospects know that a weak salesperson will fall for this every single time.

The Duck Season Rabbit Season Close - When I was a child, I was a huge fan of Bugs Bunny, simply because I thought he was a wise ass. No matter who he was facing or how many odds were stacked against him, Bugs Bunny always seemed to find a way to win.

In my humble opinion, the best Bugs Bunny cartoons were the ones where he was facing Elmer Fudd and Daffy Duck. Without a doubt, Bugs Bunny was clearly the smartest person in the Forest.

The object of this particular close is to get someone to do exactly the opposite of what they say they want to do. Bugs Bunny was an expert in getting Daffy Duck to do things he wasn't even willing to do. Here is how Bugs Bunny was able to accomplish this time and again:

Step 1. State your facts clearly, calmly and plainly; you should also be prepared to tell them that if making a purchase today is something that they're not ready to handle, you totally understand and respect that position.

Step 2. Make them realize that only the most elite, most diligent, and most intelligent people tend to act on your proposal right away. This is in no way designed to insult them, it's designed to make them think that they're missing out on something great. This is how you plant the seeds of curiosity inside their minds.

Step 3. Agree with the prospect that this is clearly not the product or service for them, then immediately ask them for their forgiveness for wasting their time. To add just enough insult to injury, ask them if they know anyone who would be willing to take action right now. This is how you plant that seed of curiosity.

Step 4. Watch them beg to be shot in the face. With this close, you have to deliver it with a certain amount of style, patience and charm. Most people don't like to be told that they can't have something, so the natural reaction is usually to get the one thing that they want, even if that means they have to change their opinion on the fly in order to save face. This is exactly what happens when Bugs Bunny goes back and forth with Daffy Duck as to whether or not it is "Duck Season" or "Rabbit Season," and we know how that ends:

With Daffy Duck having his beak blown to the back of his head. To put it another way, not only does Daffy Duck take the rifle and point it at his head, he demands that you shoot him! Yes, ladies and gentlemen, this close is an exercise in reverse psychology!

The Question Close

The reason you ask questions while closing is to make the prospect realize that they are drawing their own conclusions. After all, if the prospect can rationalize in their own mind why they are buying something, then you are no longer a salesperson. You become a consultant.

The main thing that you want to do is make sure that what you are giving them as an offer actually solves the problem.

For example, if I'm going to ask a question, the first question I'm always going to ask is:

"Tell me how this product or service is going to solve your problem."

This allows me to know if I can proceed with offering an upsell, as well as finding out if they're totally sold on what's been presented to them.

Whatever you do, under no circumstances are you to ever ask a closed-ended question. I've seen people lose sales because they got a no when they thought that they were going to get a yes. Avoid a closed-ended question like the plague. More often than not, that your sales depend on it.

The What's The Hold Up Close

This is another really good question close that automatically forces the prospect to make the sale for you in their own mind before you ever ring it up or ask for a credit card.

In a very calm and matter-of-fact tone of voice, ask the following question to the customer:

"Could you please tell me any reason why we couldn't get this done for you today."

Keep in mind that when you're at the close of the sale, the customer has already made up in their mind that they're going to go ahead and get this done. All you need to do is reinforce that line of thinking.

While other sales experts will tell you that this is a risky thing to do, I think that this question goes right to the heart of the issue. You don't ever want to waste your time with someone who was just pussyfooting or tire kicking. After all, there are too many actual buyers ready to give you their money for you to waste time with people who are "just looking".

The Serena Williams Close

I nicknamed this close after my favorite tennis player for a very specific reason: no matter what kind of way someone serves the ball at her, Serena Williams finds a way to return it to them with a lot more force and skill. Here's how it works:

Sometimes when the prospect is close to buying, they will ask a set of smokescreen questions just to nitpick or to see if they can get what they specifically want. No matter the question, swing an answer right back to them that forces them to make a decision.

Prospect: *"Does this car come in green?"*

Salesperson: *"Would you like the car to come in green?"*

Once they get tired of trying to create roadblocks between them and purchasing what they want/need from you, they will gladly buy. Just make sure that through every step of the sales process you're gauging the seriousness of the prospect.

I don't care what close you choose to use, just make sure that you ground them in your own self-confidence, product knowledge, and an unrelenting desire to get the sale no matter what the odds look like.

Here are a few brief tips that should automatically increase your closing percentage:

Listen Like you give a Damn

This would seem that it should go without saying, but

unfortunately, too many people put on their "cash ears" (listening for the ways to make money) and not their "consultative ears" (listening to add value to the customer's purchases, thereby making more money).

I get it. I really do. Most prospects tend to yak on and on about nothing of importance or relevance to you or your sales quota. I don't like pointless conversations at all. Ask any of my friends or family members, and they will tell you that I'm notorious for begging people to get to the point.

You have to realize that the "point" for you is at the end of the small talk about little Billy's cub scout troop: a sale that could lead to other sales from the other cub scout troop parents. This is a game. In order to play it well and win, you have to make sure that the prospects feel that you are dialed into them and that you are there for their every need. My dad used to say that people don't need to know how you really feel, they just need to think that you care. Who knows? Maybe not being a self-serving jackass could get you more business!

Practice?? We're Talking about PRACTICE?

Contrary to what Alan Iverson (The basketball icon

who famously fussed at reporters regarding a question about him missing practice with the Philadelphia 76'ers) may think, practicing is the key to making your entire sales process the best that it can be.

In my career, I spent countless hours practicing different ways to sell something. I experimented with different ways to talk to people, along with different intonations and pitching my voice to match the mood of the conversation I'm engaging in.

While people will tell you that it's great to practice in front of the mirror, I totally disagree with that. My http://ibranduniversity.com students know that the best "practice" you could have comes from actually selling to different people using all types of techniques until you find one (or several) that suits you.

Have you ever watched a famous stand-up comedian hold the attention of an audience for an hour and a half and wonder how they do it so effortlessly? It's most likely due to the fact that they have told a series of jokes hundreds of times in small venues, so by the time you see the routine, it's as effortless as someone saying "hello."

I've been blessed to work with some of the greatest comedians in the history of the business. My favorite comedian of all time is a man named George Wallace. I remember asking him what his writing process looked like before he hired me to write for him.

He smiled at me and said, "I do my writing for the stage, kid. If you want to find the material, the best place is in front of an audience."

Heeding that advice has yielded me hundreds of thousands of dollars throughout the course of my career. In my opinion it is true that all life is a stage and the best way to get the biggest stage of them all is through deliberate and consistent practice.

Proverbs 4:7

My favorite verse in all of the Bible says

"...and in all of thy getting, get an understanding."

This verse deals with the concept of wisdom. Have you ever studied so hard for a test that you know everything in the course material? I know that I have! However, in most cases I was simply studying the material so that I could get an A on my report card. Outside of that, I had very little interest in whatever the subject was.

I believe it is absolutely crucial to your sales career to be wise. You obviously need to be wise about your products, but more than that, you need to be wise about who you're selling what to and why.

You need to have enough sense to realize that everything will not fit everyone, but there should be something that will fit perfectly for the prospect you're serving. Selling a trumpet player a saxophone mouthpiece makes absolutely no sense. However, selling that same trumpet player a jazz mute, a mobile carrying case, and a trumpet mouthpiece designed to help him or her hit higher notes are the things that separates a wise salesperson from someone who is just trying to make the sale.

While you may think that my previous example sounds absurd, I've actually seen things like that happen.

When your main focus of selling is the sale, you miss out on very important details that can cost you money. It's not enough just to listen to what your prospect says. You have to be willing to understand and even anticipate all of their needs throughout your entire interaction. Rely on using well thought-out phrases and questions like:

"So what I hear you saying is…"

"Tell me more about…"

"Let me just make sure I understand…"

"Could you repeat that?"

"Is there anything additional that you're looking for that I haven't presented to you?"

"So tell me, what brought you here today?"

"How long have you been looking for a product or service like this one?"

The more you engage and dial in to your customer, the bigger your sales will be. People want to be sold, they just have a very hard time admitting that. The only time a person does not want to be sold is when they don't feel respected and when the product or service does not suit their needs or wants.

Throughout the sales process, you're playing two totally different roles. The first role you play is that of a student. You're there to listen, take notes and regurgitate all of the pertinent information that the prospect is giving you.

The second and most important role a salesperson can ever play is that of an educator. Your job is to make sure that your prospect has all the information at their disposal in order to make an informed and well thought-out decision. The best salespeople I know are those constantly learning so that they can become better teachers.

Closing in and of itself should be totally effortless. You should not have to beg someone nor should you have to strong-arm them into something that they want and need for themselves in order to improve their lives. If you didn't close the deal, it's due to you not providing enough information, or the prospect truly believes that your offer does not suit them.

The smart salesperson realizes that they are closing from the second they say hello. They are intuitive, understanding, and thought-provoking leaders who act as guides through the entire sales process. Don't be afraid to fail. Don't be afraid to learn. Never be afraid to ask a question, and by all means never be afraid to ask for and assume the sale.

Happy   closing!

Chapter Three
The Art of the Upsell

Most "sales experts" don't seem to think about upselling the way that I do. I teach my personal coaching students and one-on-one students at http://ibranduniversity.com all of my techniques that will add more value for their clients and more profits for them as business owners. That's not to say that I think that I'm better than those folks. I'm saying that I see an amazing value in upselling clients.

Notice that I said "clients" instead of "prospects," because at most times, the prospect has been sold some type of product or service. This is important because if a customer has already purchased from you, you've established trust and some level of rapport and respect. Not only are their hearts and minds open, but so are their wallets.

Let me give you a real world example of how an upsell works. Visit http://ibranduniversity.com/upsell and check out how I upsell people looking to take their businesses to the next level. You'll find that it's super easy and nothing to be scared about.

Why is the concept of upselling such an uncomfortable thing for most salespeople? I think it comes down to fear of losing everything by asking for more business, even if it's relatively small in comparison to the main sale. This is a critical mistake because companies with much lower cost offerings do this and it's totally revolutionizing their businesses.

In 1927, an ice store in Dallas named Southland Ice Dock made a huge change. The owner, "Uncle Johnny" Jefferson Green, had the sense to realize that people needed and wanted basic necessities long after the grocery stores closed for the night. Without hesitation, he stocked his place with eggs, milk, bread and snacks, and the convenience store was born. The Southland Ice Dock became a company you may know as 7-Eleven. Imagine an entire company built on the concept of an upsell! If you've ever had a Big Gulp or a Slurpee, you don't have to imagine at all.

When you go to a fast-food restaurant, you're being upsold with "Supersizing," dessert items and kid's toys to make your children's meals "happy." The idea of "would you like fries with that?" is as natural as breathing for most of us when we're consumers, but why not when we are merchants?

If you knew that on average, one upsell was going to make you an additional $15,000 a year in profit, isn't that worth the extra thirty seconds of time it would take to ask? You've already pitched! You've already closed! What's one more question mean to you? The answer is that it means everything to you if it increases your bottom line!

What's the easiest way to upsell a client? Simply continue the conversation. At this point you should have more than enough discovery information to know their likes or dislikes. You should be able to say something like this:

Salesperson: *"So, now that you've agreed to having your kitchen floor done, did you know that we can get your cabinets done for you, completely installed for an additional $2 day?"*

Client: *"That would be awesome! Let's do it!!"*

While $730 on top of a $5000 sale might seem like a drop in the bucket, if you did that for twenty customers a year, that's an additional $14,600 in revenue that you wouldn't have made without asking.

With the previous example, the salesperson explained the benefits of redoing the cabinets in a roundabout way. What was implied was that the client's new floor would be even more spectacular when complemented by fresh, new cabinets. Sometimes you need to be more direct with your explanation. Feel your customer out and understand your level of connection with your client.

The Upsell in Real Life

Let's stop talking about selling for a minute and let's just talk about our lives in general. I recall going to the beauty store with my wife, Janay (who's the one who arguably should be writing this book because she's sold me on so many things I had no desire to buy, LOL), and she seemed to be having trouble trying to decide which shampoo to purchase.

Being the good husband that I am, I asked Janay what her dilemma was.

Standing there with two different brands of shampoo in her hands, she looked up at me and said, *"Both of these shampoos are good, but this one is better, but it's going to cost twenty percent more. I don't know if it's worth it."*

As a man, I really don't care about the cost of shampoo. As a husband, I care only about my wife's happiness and total satisfaction at all costs. Without batting an eye, I sprang into action.

"*Honey*," I said, *"you only get one head of hair and you want to make sure you take the best care of it. If that means I have to pay an additional twenty percent for better shampoo, that's what's going to have to happen."*

She then flashed that gorgeous million-dollar smile of hers and said, *"You're right, honey!"*

The next thing I knew, we're walking out of the damned beauty supply store with all types of gel and hair products and oils, the names of most of which I couldn't even pronounce.

What Janay wound up doing was something I do to prospects every single day and they never see it coming. She gave me two very viable options, made the case for value above cost, and then forced me into a position where I advocated for why I needed to pay more for something.

Because I'd just finished advocating for why cost should not stand in the way of proper hair care, my wife walked out with every single hair product she felt she needed. I couldn't very well go back on what I said because I would look like a hypocrite. After all, did I not just finish saying to her that she only gets "one head of hair"?

I still don't know whether I was manipulated or if my wife genuinely needed my help. What I do know is that she and the store clerk were very happy with my purchases.

As I write this I feel more like a sucker. LOL.

Children are arguably the greatest salespeople ever in the history of mankind. My oldest daughter, Midori, can make a case for something that she wants that is so solid and airtight that I think even the late Johnnie Cochran would not be able to combat it.

"Dad, if I have the HD cable box in my room with on-demand capabilities, I wouldn't always be in the living room or in your and Mom's room. It's only an additional twelve dollars a month to the cable bill, and you and Mom can spend more quality time together alone."

You would think that this would've been the best $12 that I spent in my entire life. You would be wrong. Midori loves to be in our room and in the living room even though I caved in and got her exactly what she wanted. What can I say? The kid loves being around her parents… and the sixty inch big screen in the living room. In all fairness, she does spend quite a bit of time in her room by herself watching the cable. I just don't know if I can attribute that to the quality of cable she has available to her in her room or if it's just good old-fashioned teenage angst.

Take a look at your own life for a moment. How many times has a loved one or a good friend got you to buy into an idea that you weren't particularly sold on in the beginning? Some would argue that you did it out of love, while I contend that you did it because there was an argument that you were open to hearing, and your sense of logic prevailed. This is exactly what you need to do when you're upselling your customers.

All you need to do is present the facts, apply logic and promote the value. Now I'm not going to pretend that there are subtle nuances and every type of upselling experience. I am going to say that over time, you are more than capable of mastering all of those nuances.

If a particular sales process was a hard one, you might want to forgo the upsell. If you felt like it was easy then you might want to go for the gusto! You have to read mood as well as factor in how much time you spent, what level of rapport you've established, and if you've done a good enough job of educating your client.

Respect the NO

Some customers might not want to spend beyond what they've already allocated. That's okay. Just don't be pushy. I've seen salespeople lose previously closed deals by being too pushy. It's okay to ask the question. It's not okay to keep bugging your client after the sale. You should know when a "no" is an actual NO vs. a "Tell me more."

Quarters are better than Dollars.

As a rule of thumb, you should never try to sell anything that would cost more than 25% of the total cost of the main sale. There's got to be a very good reason for a big upsell. The reason doesn't necessarily have to make sense to you, but you have to make it realistic for your customer.

If you increase the cost of an average sale by 25%, your profits will soar higher than you ever thought possible! If you're able to increase the bottom line by 25% you'll not only create more value, but you'll give the customer the feeling of marquis level customer service.

Don't Judge a Book by Its Cover

You can never make the mistake of assuming that you know what's in your customers' wallets. Trust me when I say you don't have a clue. I have walked into several establishments looking to spend my hard-earned money, only to be ignored and/or dismissed.

Most millionaires I know are either horrible dressers or they don't care enough to put that much thought into their clothing on a daily basis. Either way, you do not know where your next sale is coming from or how much money you're missing out on because of your ignorant prejudices.

In August 2013, Oprah Winfrey, one of the richest women on the face of the earth (at the time I'm writing this, Oprah Winfrey has a net worth of approximately $3 billion), happened to be shopping in Switzerland, looking for a gift for Tina Turner's wedding.

She found herself in a store that sold all types of designer handbags. In her own words, Oprah recounted what happened next:

"I was in Zürich the other day, and the store's name I will not mention. I didn't have my eyelashes on, but I was in full Oprah Winfrey gear. I have my little Donna Karan skirt and my little sandals. But obviously, the Oprah Winfrey show is not shown in Zürich. I go into a store and say to the woman, 'Excuse me, may I see the bag right above your head?' And she says to me, 'No, it's too expensive.'"

In recalling the story to Larry King, Oprah mused that she thought about buying out the entire store just to prove a point, but thought better of it because the last thing she wanted to do was reward prejudice and ignorance with a higher commission.

Can you imagine such ignorance? Can you imagine how much money that prejudiced store clerk missed out on? Let's say that $42,000 purse came with a 10% commission for that clerk. That's $4,200! More than they average American makes in a month!

If that clerk had treated Oprah like a valued customer, even if she had never previously stepped foot into that establishment, you know there could have been a couple of quick, "no brainer" upsells. With a handbag, there's a change purse, a handbag organizer, a handheld compact mirror and makeup case, etc. That ignorant (and in my opinion, idiotic) clerk could have easily turned $42,000 into $50,000 without doing a bit of heavy lifting!

Now let's add in the "Oprah effect"! Say that in an alternate universe this transaction, upsells included went off without a hitch. You know Oprah has a "favorite things" list that can turn an obscure product/service into a multimillion dollar "must have" item overnight! Factor that in along with the power of social media and Oprah's pleasant experience with that particular clerk and that lady could have had a private jet and an accompanying island by now! I may be exaggerating, but not by much!

Now how much money have you missed by thinking that someone wasn't capable of affording your product or service?

Everyone brings their experiences and their prejudices into their job. Unfortunately, we high-performing salespeople know that the only time it's appropriate to judge anyone is when their check bounces or their credit card declines. Money is green. It doesn't care who holds it. It never asks about an education level or the type of household you were brought up in. Money is the biggest equalizer in most cases, and while many people treat money with respect, we need to go out of our way to do the same for the people who hold the purse strings.

Look for the Unspoken Opportunities to Upsell

When I'm selling to someone face-to-face, I watch everything they do. I also pay attention to what they say. The most telling information you can ever get from a prospect comes from their body language.

Watch what their eyes seem to gravitate toward when you're with them. Notice little things about them physically. If it's a man, take a look at his hands to see if they are well manicured. If they are, it's a good chance that he takes care of himself and takes extra pride in his appearance. It's a slight stereotype, but men with manicures tend to spend more than those who have dirt under their nails. Like I said earlier, some people fake the funk, so be very careful with stereotypes.

If you see a woman who you can tell works a lot, she may enjoy the opportunity to pamper herself. There's a good chance you can play up the idea of giving herself something that she "deserves." A once-in-a-while type of treat can lead to bigger commissions for you.

One thing that I do a lot if I'm selling someone face-to-face is pay attention to those they have around them. You can tell a lot by the people that someone associates themselves with on a shopping excursion. Sometimes the easiest way to upsell someone is to ask their friends or companions what they think of a good upsell.

Let's just say you're selling jeans, for example. If you sold a prospect two pairs of jeans, a dark wash pair and another that was a standard wash, you might ask their friend, *"What do you think about getting your friend a black pair to go along with these two?"*

At this point you can allow your friend you are the advocating for you while you continue to ring up the sale.

Stop Being Afraid of the Money

The numbers say it all: anywhere from 30% to 67% of consumers who buy something are ready, willing and able to be upsold. These people are already in a buying mood, so what do you expect? Do you think that they're going to say no to you?

Let's say that someone does say no to you when you offer an upsell. What's the worst thing that's going to happen? They could say no, but statistics show that the average person will not say no to you BECAUSE THEY'VE ALREADY SAID YES!! So basically you're allowing money to walk out of the door based on nothing but fear of rejection.

Let me try to put this another way: if you've already asked a very attractive person out on a date and they said yes, and that date goes well, what's the harm in asking them for a nightcap? Other than the fact that you may be moving a little too fast for their comfort level, you closed the deal the second they agreed to go out with you. This is just taking things to a new level. Whether you choose to believe this or not, I promise you that an upsell is no more difficult than asking somebody out on a date, after you've already had a great date.

To allow someone to leave without getting them to buy everything we possibly can when they're in a buying mood, is only doing a disservice to yourself and your bottom line. The top performing sales reps in the world are not afraid to go the extra mile and ask for the upsell. Only those of us who are scared and ruled by our emotions will miss out on this tremendous opportunity to increase our income and make already happy clients even happier!

Chapter Four
Repeat, Repeat, Repeat!

One thing that people miss out on quite frequently, that is the easiest thing in the world to get, is repeat business.

Too many times in business, both large corporations and small mom and pop businesses try to focus on customer acquisition as opposed to customer retention. Now, while customer acquisition is a big part of business, having repeat business means that you can factor in a growth in your bottom line year-over-year. This is especially true if you're offering awesome customer service for your loyal patrons.

According to Bain & Company, it costs on average six to seven times more to get a new customer as opposed to just hanging on to one who has already shown some level of brand loyalty and awareness.

Let's not stop there! If you look at recent statistics for Marketing Metrics, you have a better shot of selling something to someone who's already an existing customer! From a financial perspective, the odds of selling to a person who has already patronized your business are in your favor. How much are they in your favor? Try a whopping 60 to 70%!

Conversely, the odds of you selling to a new prospect are a dismal 5 to 20%. Now let me ask you, which one of those odds makes the most sense for you to bank your efforts on consistently?

If you've ever seen the movie, Tyler Perry's *Why Did I Get Married?*, there's a poignant scene where the cast members are talking about what's referred to as the 80/20 rule. They were talking about how a spouse will give you about 80% of what you'll need, while that extra 20% is the unknown part that excites you, leading people to cheat.

The 80/20 rule that I'm referring to states that if you nurture, cultivate, and ultimately love your clients and customers with loyalty, specials, and respect for their time and dollar, 20% of all the people that you will serve will make up 80% of your profits!

If you still think that this isn't enough reason to focus on repeat customers, let me try a few more things that will wow you:

With repeat business, those customers and clients know what to expect from you, your company, and the brand that you represent. You don't have to spend time and valuable resources trying to educate them about how great you are! If you sell yourself right the first time as a business, a salesperson, or an organization, you'll never have to worry. There will be no such thing as a down economy for you and your business. Simply put, if you do your job right the first time, you never have to worry about doing it again.

With repeat customers, you never have to worry about building trust. In the mind of the repeat customer, you're already the expert in whatever it is that you sell to them. When it comes to new customers, until you have proven yourself worthy, you're nothing more than an order taker and a business that is just auditioning for the expert status in the life of that particular patron.

So now you're asking, *"How in the world do I make these people repeat customers?"*

Great question! Here's what I believe in doing:

First you need to learn the names of your customers. If you're in retail, make yourself a note of the top five people who come and patronize your business. Keep a notebook of what it is they purchase, and see if you can get their phone number so that you can alert them of what's coming up.

If you're in the online marketing world, you need to at all costs develop a strong and consistent email list. Tools like MailChimp are godsends for people who are trying to keep in touch with a customer base. Along those lines, make sure that you send people online coupons that they can use and also share with their friends on social media. Those are things that are going to allow you to get people in the door. Also keep in mind that when you issue a discount or a coupon, it will automatically pay for itself the second you get business that you would not have had if you had not issued that coupon in the first place.

The one thing that drives people crazy about my sales strategies is that I love to over deliver. Does that mean that I'm perfect? No! It does mean that I try my best to make things happen for customers, to the point where they can't stop raving about me and the service that I give them.

In Nashville, Tennessee, there's a restaurant I like to go to called The Mellow Mushroom. The Mellow Mushroom is a pizza joint that serves amazing drinks and arguably has some of the best pizza I've ever had in my entire life!

What I love about their service is that if they have something new on the menu, they have no problem giving you free samples. If you've had way too many of their strong electric lemonade drinks, they will try to sober you up with free breadsticks and even call you a taxi cab. No matter where I go, I will always compare pizza joints to The Mellow Mushroom because I have never experienced that level of service at any other pizza joint as long as I've been eating pizza.

It's one thing to be consultative, it's another thing entirely to treat your customer as if you are their own personal concierge service. To be able to anticipate a need that the customer has yet to think of puts you in the upper echelon of people in their life, both personally and professionally.

About a year ago I went to a store called Destination XL. Because I'm a big man, I have to be very carefulof where I shop for clothing. After undergoing a very painful surgery, I was stuck with a catheter for period of two weeks while I healed. This meant that I needed something to wear that was not going to be restrictive by any far stretch of the imagination.

When I entered the store, a smiling man named Mike came and greeted my wife and me with a smile and two bottles of ice cold water on a hot summer day. We explained to him my situation and what we were looking for. And for the next hour, this man rolled out the red carpet and even helped me dress myself when I couldn't function fully on my own.

By the time he walked us to the register, I was completely sold. Mike even went as far as to give me his business card, which had his cell phone number on it, and told me that if I found something somewhere that I was interested in to call him first so he could order it in my size. He then went on to inform my wife that he had taken my measurements and would keep them on file so that if she ever wanted to surprise me with a gift, he could have it perfectly fitted for me.

In the event that something I purchased at his store did not fit the way that I wanted it, he would have his personal tailor make alterations for me free of charge. I do not know how many thousands of dollars I have spent at Destination XL because Mike has gone out of his way for me. Furthermore, when it comes to all of my friends who are big men, without hesitation I send them right to Mike so that they can experience this awesome service that I've been getting.

Don't ever be afraid to ask for criticism or different ways that you would be able to improve your customer's experience for them. Your customers are always going to tell you the truth, especially if you treat them with respect.

Also, remember that customers who give you feedback are a free focus group for you. They can tell you what you're doing right, and they can also tell you what you're doing wrong. Both sets of information are extremely valuable. Make sure you reward them by giving them a discount, some kind of coupon, or some kind of free gift that will ensure that they feel good about giving you their business consistently.

One more thing about email lists:

You'll be surprised how one particular thing can get you more loyalty than anything you've ever done in sales. If you don't pay attention to anything else in this book, pay attention to this! I've arguably saved my best secret for last.

Are you ready?

When you ask people to sign up for your email list, also ask them for their birthday. This is important, because you can send them something exclusivel under birthday that no one else can get. This thing, this birthday gift that you're giving them, needs to be substantial in order to have maximum impact.

In case you are wondering what I'm suggesting here, my rule of thumb is to give people 40% off on their birthday. While people will tell you that that is a lot of money to give away, look at it this way:

There aren't too many people are going to have the same birthday, and 40% off for one customer who is going to be a brand ambassador for you is a very sound investment. People love getting stuff for free or at an extreme discount just by virtue of the fact that they were born. Yes, it is appealing to their ego, but who gives a rat's ass? It is smart business! Whether some people feel like it is a cheap trick or not, it puts butts in seats and money in your purse. To me, that's all that needs to be said!

Epilogue

I have to be very direct and honest with you—the world of sales is not for everyone. Some people can't handle the pressure, while other people have issues with rejection. Some people can't do well with sales quotas, while others can't take the problems that come with needy customers, tire kickers, and price gougers.

If you're able to master the ability to control yourself, your emotions, your prejudices and your shortcomings, you'll find that there is no job more rewarding if you're willing to give it your all.

While I've held many different jobs and worn many different hats, aside from being a husband and a father, I've enjoyed nothing more than mastering my personal approach to salesmanship.

I wrote this book so that you would have a guide as to how you should conduct yourself in the sales arena. I wasn't trying to write a sales bible. I wanted to write a book that was going to make sales approachable for anyone, regardless of their previous experiences in sales.

It is my sincere wish that you take from this book the insights and ideas that work best for you and your personal sales technique. I want you to enjoy selling as much as you enjoy making or providing whatever service or product you offer to the world.

I totally believe that you can sell anything if you're given the right circumstances. The most important thing that you'll ever selling your entire life is yourself.

Thanks for reading this book. It means the world to me that you even bothered to pick it up.

If you're interested in working with me, you can sign up for my iBrand University course at http://ibranduniversity.com

For personal coaching, speaking and press requests, feel free to call the office at (929) 35-BRAND

Happy selling!

Dave Anderson
info@innerbrand.org

P.S. I welcome feedback and questions, so please don't hesitate to shoot me an email. I promise to answer every single email I get!

Acknowledgments

I'm nothing without my faith, so I would first like to acknowledge my Lord and Savior, Jesus Christ.

I know that people say that at award ceremonies and when it's convenient or cute, but if you'd been through what I've been through, you would know that my praise is real, unwavering and full of gratitude.

Second only to God himself is the greatest sales accomplishment of my life, my amazing and supportive wife, Janay. The day that I met you, I told you that I was going to be your husband, and although you told me that I was crazy, you're here! It took me fifteen years to "close" you, but I think it is safe to say that you're sold on me. Your love is one of the principal reasons that this book exists. I'm grateful for your many gifts and sacrifices for our marriage and our family.

I've been everywhere, and I can't think of anyone who comes close to you. No matter what happens, know that you are my best friend and the greatest companion anyone could ask for in the journey we call life.

To my two beautiful girls, Midori and Devlyn, know that Daddy works every day to be worthy of your unconditional love. Thanks for understanding those moments when I couldn't be there right away, and those times were couldn't get you everything that you wanted and deserved.

While I can never make up for those moments that I missed out on while writing this book, know that you two are my main reasons why I get up in the morning and go to war with the craziness of life on earth. You are both so bright and beautiful. I wish you both success and the ability to see in the mirror the greatness I see when I look at you.

To my mother, thanks for having me. That was pretty flipping awesome of you. Thanks for challenging me as a kid. You're arguably the first person I've ever sold on anything, and whether it was to build my self-esteem or I was just that good, you made me believe in the impossible.

Your sacrifices are too numerous to count, but I thank you for all of them.

To my late father, Carl Anderson, your teachings and love still resonate with me over a decade after your passing. I saw the world, met a great girl and gave you two grandchildren. I'm drug and disease free and I help people every day to be the best version of themselves. I'm a flawed man, Dad, but I try hard every day to get it right. I will always love you because it was you who told me that it was possible to do absolutely anything. I'm happy to say that you were right!

Thanks to my brother, Aaron, for being an awesome

example of how a man should behave in a dark and difficult millennium. I know I don't get to see you very much because our schedules don't line up, but I'm so happy to say that I'm the kid brother to a real-life hero!

Thanks for getting me things that Mom couldn't afford so that I wouldn't be laughed at in school. Thanks for bullying the kids who bullied me so the next time, they'd have to find another victim. Thanks for showing me how to survive. Most of all, thanks for teaching me the importance of self-sacrifice.

You have a wonderful family. To Trish, Kiarra and AJ, I love you and I hope you're still pushing to fulfill your own unique paths.

To my cousin Brie, I love you, and for as long as I can remember, it's been me and you. You are more than a cousin, you're a sister and I love you dearly.

To my Aunt Gigi, I love you for every beautiful gift you've brought into my life. Your support has been life altering.

Thanks to my in-laws for always believing in me. It's rare that people have such good relationships with the family that they married into, so I am grateful to no end for your love and support.

To Loraine Ballard Morrill, you never turned your back on me and I will never forget that. Thank you.

To TeeJ Mercer, you're a true unicorn. Thank you for reminding me that the world can be a ((shudders)) "yummy and delicious" place! #episode (LOL).

To Ahmir Young and http://egrassrootsbusiness.com thank you for being there and for all of the countless things you've done for me, both known and unknown.

Thanks to all of my friends and family from all aspects of my life. Because I've shouted you out in every other book, you should know that I love you and I'm grateful.

Subsequently, if any one of you bastards comes to me asking why I didn't shout you out in this book, I want you to read this clearly:

MY BRAIN IS FRIED FROM SPENDING MONTHS TRYING TO FIND A WAY TO TAKE MY WACKY SALES PROCESS OUT OF MY BIG ASS HEAD AND TRANSPOSE IT TO PAPER! WHEN YOU SEE ME, HAND ME THE BOOK AND I WILL SIGN IT WITH A PERSONAL DEDICATION, ACKNOWLEDGING HOW MUCH YOU MEAN TO ME. IN THE MEANTIME, ACCEPT THE DAMN THANK YOU AND ENJOY THE BOOK!

Made in the USA
San Bernardino, CA
07 May 2017